BEHOLD THE WORD

52 visual meditations

BEHOLD THE WORD

52 visual meditations

by
James Roose-Evans

with painted inscriptions by
John Rowlands-Pritchard

redemptorist
publications

Redemptorist Publications
Wolf's Lane, Chawton, Hampshire, GU34 3HQ, UK
Tel. +44 (0)1420 88222, Fax. +44 (0)1420 88805
Email rp@rpbooks.co.uk, www.rpbooks.co.uk

A registered charity limited by guarantee
Registered in England 03261721

Edited by Katharine Stockermans
Designed by Eliana Thompson

ISBN 978-0-85231-597-2

Scripture quotations from The Authorized (King James) Version. Rights in the Authorized Version in the United Kingdom are vested in the Crown. Reproduced by permission of the Crown's patentee, Cambridge University Press.

A CIP catalogue record for this book is available from the British Library.

Printed by Bishops Printers, Portsmouth, PO6 1TR

For Dame Philippa Edwards OSB of Stanbrook Abbey,

with love and gratitude for years of friendship and prayer.

Foreword
by James Roose-Evans

Words carved in stone, painted on wood, canvas or paper are for me words carved in the heart. I have never forgotten how, each time I came out of our village church in the Forest of Dean, carved on the first tombstone by the porch I would see the words: "In memory of Josiah Trump who awaits the last Trump". It struck me as a rare example of grave humour!

Years later, when I was twenty-one, I used to serve Mass once a week at the Carmelite Monastery in Bridge Lane, Golders Green. After Mass the two extern sisters would take me to a parlour where there was a table spread with a starched linen tablecloth and shining plates; even the slabs of butter had moisture on them like dewdrops, and a plate of fried bacon, eggs and mushrooms. Those silent breakfasts were indeed very special. Then a bell would ring to signal for me to go to another parlour for a talk with the Prioress, Sister Anne of the Holy Spirit, who had taken me under her wing. This was 1949 so there was not only a formidable heavy iron grille between myself and the Prioress but also her face was always covered with a black veil. On one occasion she showed me some photographs of the interior of the monastery. One that made a great impression on me was of an arch. Painted around it were the words: "In Carmel and at the Judgement I am alone." I thought about what an impact these words must make on the nuns as they passed them many times during each day. A few words singled out in this way make a greater impact than many words on page after page.

It was in 1980 that in a London gallery I saw, mounted and framed, some words of a poem penned in a way I had never seen before. I bought it and learned it was by John Rowlands-Pritchard who was a lay vicar choral at Wells Cathedral and lived in the close with his wife Mary and their son. I visited him and we became friends. Shortly after that I invited him to give an exhibition of his work at the Old School Gallery in Bleddfa, a small hamlet in Radnorshire, on the borders of Wales, where I had founded the Bleddfa Trust as a Centre for the Creative Spirit in 1974. Then in 1988 John founded Opus Anglicanum, which has done so much over the past three decades to restore interest in Gregorian chant through their performances and workshops in cathedrals and churches throughout the country.

I invited them to perform at Bleddfa first in 1992, then in 2002 and 2004, and on other occasions since, as well as hosting further exhibitions of John's work. Over the years I would commission him to paint certain phrases or sentences that were meaningful to me on canvas or paper, and these hang on every wall of my home. I had cards made of them so that I could share them with friends.

So, what is the appeal? It is the daily seeing of such texts that causes them to sink deep into one's subconscious like the repetition of a mantra, or the regular praying of the rosary. Now, in my ninety-third year, it seemed appropriate to share his work with many others and I am delighted that Redemptorist Publications have made it possible for you to see at least some of John Rowlands-Pritchard's work with my short meditations accompanying them.

In this collection you will find one meditation for each week of the year. It is not a book to be raced through in one reading and then put aside! Rather it reminds me of one of the most original books I have ever read. Entitled *The Book of Books*, it was by the Sufi master Idries Shah. It tells the story of a wise man who taught his disciples from a seemingly inexhaustible store of wisdom. He attributed all his knowledge to a thick book which was kept in a place of honour in his room and which he would allow no one to open. After his death the book was handed down from one generation to another. It came to be known as *The Book of Books*. By now I had reached page eleven, and it is at this point that Idries Shah tells the reader that in the pages that follow we shall find the content of *The Book of Books*. There then follow 260 pages of thick, white, entirely blank paper! Each of those pages I "read" slowly. I knew enough of Sufi teaching jokes to be aware that they are meant to be taken as seriously as any *koan* in Zen. I could easily have cheated, whipping through the pages, nodding sagely and saying, "Yes, I get the point!" Instead I slowly turned blank page after blank page, absorbing the impression of each. The "reading" of those pages remains to this day a rich and instructive experience for me. At the end I wrote some words from an early Buddhist text on the final page: "The truth was never preached by the Buddha, seeing that you have to realise it within yourself."

•   •   •

I am reminded of some words of that remarkable young woman Etty Hillesum who died at Auschwitz. In an early diary she wrote:

> Looked at Japanese prints this afternoon. That's how I want to write. With that much space round a few words. They should simply emphasise the silence – the few great things that matter in life can be said in a few words… What matters is the right relationship between words and wordlessness, the wordlessness in which much more happens than in all the words one can string together.

And so it is my hope that each reader will take time to absorb and meditate on each of the phrases or sentences so visualised in this collection.

London, 2020

Those who live in the countryside know how some nights are so dark – no glimpse of the moon, nor stars – and yet if we walk outside we become aware of life all around: the hoot of an owl, the squeak of a small shrew caught, the shuffling of a hedgehog, the murmur of roosting birds, and above all we sense the sap rising in trees and plants. Life goes on, day in, day out, season by season. We know that, however dark the night, daylight will come and a new day will dawn.

So, too, in our lives: whatever darkness of failure, betrayal, loss of a job, or illness overwhelms us, something new will dawn in us. Even the helpless victim of a hopeless situation may rise above herself. Viktor Frankl, in *Man's Search for Meaning*, tells the story of Jerry Long who was paralysed from the neck down in a diving accident which rendered him a quadriplegic at the age of seventeen. In a letter to Frankl he wrote:

> I view my life as being abundant with meaning and purpose. The attitude that I adopted on that fateful day has become my personal credo for life. I broke my neck, it didn't break me. I am currently enrolled on my first psychology course in college. I believe that my handicap will only enhance my ability to help others. I know that without the suffering, the growth that I have achieved would have been impossible.

At midnight noon is born.

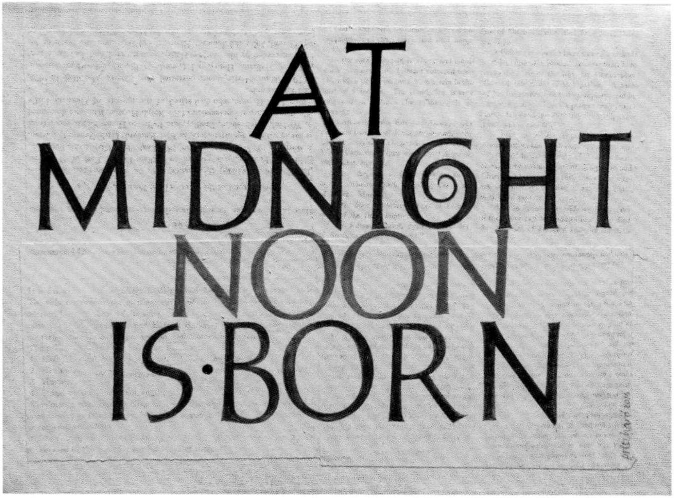
AT
MIDNIGHT
NOON
IS·BORN

It frequently happens, especially among men, that around the age of forty there is a midlife crisis, when the individual finds that the job he has been pursuing is not fulfilling, however much money is being earned. There is a sense that one's life must be about something more. I am reminded of one friend who, at the age of forty-five, went off for five years to train as a Jungian analyst and for the second half of his life became a richly gifted one. As the performer Joyce Grenfell once said, "I am less and less interested in being Joyce Grenfell than in becoming the person God wants me to be."

The most dramatic example of this that I have encountered was that of Neville Dewis who was resident stage designer of the Salisbury Playhouse in the 1970s. One day, seated on a hilltop, he thought, "Do I want to go on churning out sets every three weeks for the rest of my life?" It was then that the word "soil" came into his mind. He gave up his job at the theatre, bought a bicycle and became a jobbing gardener for about fourteen houses. He averagely earned the modest sum of about £100 a week but was one of the most contented people I have ever met.

For women the crisis can often come later, especially if they have borne children. It is when the children have grown up and left home that some women find they lose their central role as a mother. We have to be open to change.

I HAVE ALWAYS
KNOWN THAT AT
LAST I WOULD
TAKE THIS ROAD
BUT YESTERDAY
I DID NOT KNOW
THAT IT WOULD
BE TODAY

NARIHIRA

pritchard 2018

This is one of the sayings of Rumi, the great Sufi mystic and poet, and it brings to mind the great lesson of St Thomas Aquinas which the Church has never fully grasped.

On 12 December 1273 in Naples, the great theologian Thomas Aquinas had a vision while celebrating Mass, the details of which he never revealed. But from that day forward Aquinas, who had authored more than forty books, never wrote another word, but devoted himself to prayer until he died a few months later. Until then he had been engaged in his greatest work, the *Summa Theologica*, but when his spiritual director urged him to complete it, he replied, "After what I have seen, all that I have written seems like straw." Why did this prodigy, not yet fifty, so abruptly abandon the crowning achievement of his life's work? Clearly what he came to perceive is that the essence of things is beyond the reach of the rational mind.

If we stay in the root of our being and listen to the silence within, we shall intuit truths which are beyond the reach of science or intellect. It is no wonder that Jesus urged us to become as little children who have an instinctive grasp of the essentials until education starts to corrode them. I remember vividly a small boy once saying to me with great passion, "God is a *feel*, not a think!"

3

STAY IN THE
ROOT·OF·YOUR
BEING:DON'T
CLIMB·OUT·ON
INTELLECTUAL
BRANCHES:

For thousands of years all the great religions believed in winged messengers: creatures of light, who commute between heaven and earth, as in Jacob's vision of a ladder with angels descending and ascending. Muhammad too had such a vision. The angel is the voice of inner authority and cannot be disobeyed. We hear the beat of wings, sense a presence in our midst, and know we are not alone. The veil that divides this world from the next is almost transparent at such moments.

The Christian tradition says that when we are born a special angel is chosen to accompany us. This is our guardian angel who is right beside us even if, like Tobias, we don't recognise who it is. Our angel has a special responsibility to watch over us and keep a circle of light around us. I became most deeply aware of this when I was diagnosed with cancer of the thyroid and warned by the physician that my voice might be reduced to a whisper. I was filled with fear. Then one night I woke to hear an inner voice saying: "You are not alone. You have an angel working beside you." From then on all fear vanished.

BEHOLD
I SEND MY ANGEL
BEFORE YOU TO
GUARD YOU ON
YOUR WAY GIVE
HEED TO HIM AND
HEAR HIS VOICE

These words of Rilke to a young poet remind us also that the two central commands of Jesus are that we should love God with our whole heart, and our neighbour as ourselves. There are, of course, many different kinds of love: parental, maternal, paternal, sibling, fraternal, romantic, spousal, platonic, love of nature, and divine love. But it is through our human relationships that we begin to glimpse something of the love of God.

Today, sadly, statistics show that over fifty per cent of first marriages end in the seventh or eighth year, often leaving small children psychologically damaged. What is not realised is that falling in love is easy but being in love is hard work! Yet if we learn to patiently work our way through the many vicissitudes that are inevitable in a committed relationship, we shall grow into a deeper understanding of the nature of love and how it relates to others. Our love should not be ingrowing but always, always, flow out to others.

FOR ONE · HUMAN
BEING · TO · LOVE
ANOTHER · IS · THE
MOST · DIFFICULT
TASK · THAT · HAS
BEEN · ENTRUSTED
TO · US · THE · ULTIMATE
TASK · THE · FINAL
TEST · AND · PROOF

This is an old Irish blessing. One can imagine it being said to a young person leaving home and setting out on their life's journey, not knowing what lies ahead. Whatever job we apply ourselves to, the blessing reminds us that we each have another life that has to be cultivated – the interior life, which sadly too many neglect.

We are, each of us, full of contradictions and many moods, and our task is to integrate these opposites, to tame our own wild wolf, and kiss the leper, as in the stories of St Francis and as Jesus did in those forty days in the desert when we read that he was alone with wild beasts. Doubtless there really were wild animals but it refers also to his own inner fears and complexes which he had to work his way through before being able to set out on his life's true mission. The last two words of this blessing don't mean "goodbye", but rather "may you travel well", as the expression "goodbye" was originally "God be with you".

MAY THE STARS
LIGHT YOUR
WAY AND MAY
YOU FIND THE
INTERIOR
ROAD
FARE
WELL

These words of Joseph Campbell remind us once again that we are never alone. Here the story of Dr Eben Alexander, an eminent American neurosurgeon, is deeply significant. In his first book, *Proof of Heaven,* he describes how in 2008 he fell into a coma after suffering a rare form of bacterial meningitis. Scans of his brain revealed massive damage. He was not expected to survive. As his family prepared themselves for the worst, something miraculous occurred. His brain went from total inactivity to awakening. He woke a changed man, certain of the infinite reach of the soul, certain of a life beyond death. It is in his second book, *The Map of Heaven,* that he echoes the words of Joseph Campbell when he writes, "We have other family: beings who are watching and looking out for us: beings who are waiting to help us navigate our time here on earth: none of us is ever unloved." These guardians may appear in dreams, or in individuals who suddenly appear in our lives when most needed.

ONE·HAS·ONLY
TO·KNOW·AND
TRUST·AND
THE·AGELESS
GUARDIANS
WILL·APPEAR

pritchard 2015

For so many today the word "God" has become a stumbling block because of the centuries-old depiction of God as an old man with a long beard, a young man at his side and a bird hovering overhead. These are all anthropomorphic images, projections on our part, for as the great thirteenth-century mystic Meister Eckhart wrote, "God is no thing", just as Thomas Aquinas wrote, "What God is we cannot know."

Matters also have not been helped by the mistranslation of the word that Jesus uses when speaking of God. The word "Abba" does not mean "father". It is an Aramaic word, which was the language Jesus and his contemporaries mainly spoke, which means parents, mother and father. It also carries the meaning "source and origin of all things". It was Pope John Paul I who, in one of his Saturday morning addresses, said: "We have to learn to address God as Mother as well as Father, to be able to say: Our Mother who art in Heaven." This was such a comfort to countless women who for centuries had faced a steep wall of patriarchy.

God is beyond our comprehension, the unnameable, and yet we need images to help us. For me, God is like an ocean of love in which, "we live and move and have our being". As St Augustine wrote, "God is closer to me than I am to myself."

It is very revealing to observe how people shake hands and what it tells us about them. The playwright Sir James Barrie, who was deeply introverted, on meeting someone, would take their hand briefly then push it back to the other person, as though saying, "I am pleased to meet you but don't come any closer!" A true handshake is indeed an opening of our hearts to another, expressing affection, even love, welcoming the individual into our lives, into our home. This is what Jesus means when he says, "Love your neighbour as yourself."

WITH·MY·HAND
I·GREET·YOU·
IN·MY·HAND·IS
MY·HEART·IN
MY·HEART·IS
MY·LOVE·COME
INTO·MY·HOME·
COME·INTO·MY
HEART:

I AM THE WAY – WALK ME
I AM THE SONG – SING ME
I AM THE LIFE – LIVE ME

These words are based on those of Jesus who invites us to follow him. He himself is the way; we have only to walk in his footsteps, and as we go we whistle his song of love, and in so doing discover that he is indeed the source of life, that he lives in us. Jesus, on meeting the fishermen James and John, said, "Follow me!" and at once they left their nets and followed. It is as simple as that!

:I·AM·THE·WAY:
WALK·ME:

:I·AM·THE·SONG:
SING·ME:

:I·AM·THE·LIFE:
LIVE·ME:

I don't know the origin of this phrase but it is one that I have lived by — although sometimes the net *doesn't* appear and one has an almighty crash! Nonetheless, it can lead to many discoveries and a richly fulfilled life. Whether we fall in love or follow a hunch, we have to take risks. We may be in a highly successful and financially rewarding job when suddenly there comes the realisation that we are called to do something entirely different, perhaps to work for a particular charity, to retrain as a therapist, become ordained or have a call to the religious life.

Many, however, cling to the present and refuse the invitation to change, to grow, and so, born millionaires, they often die paupers. As Joanna Trollope wrote in her novel *The Rector's Wife*, "so many lack the capacity to live life richly". Each of us comes into this world with a blueprint of the person we are meant to be. The tragedy of so many lives is that people do not live their lives to the full. Most live in a waking sleep but, with work, it is possible to achieve our full potential. As the writer Katherine Mansfield wrote in the last months of her life, "I want to be what I am becoming. One rows one's boat into the darkness. If only one can accept, there is a landscape to be discovered, to be one's true self, to be afraid of nothing."

These words came to me many years ago in meditation and I invited John Rowlands-Pritchard to paint them for me. They now hang on my bedroom wall so that I see them on waking and on going to sleep. We each make our own journey into God.

The infinity of God is such that all words fail before the Ultimate Silence of the Divine. We are simply told to be still and know. These are words that our meditation group repeats aloud before commencing a thirty-minute silence. First we say, "Be still and know that I am God." There is a pause and then, "Be still and know that I am." Another pause and then, "Be still and know." Pause and, "Be still", and finally just, "Be!"

All who kneel before the Blessed Sacrament experience this depth of silence, the journey into God.

GOD·IS·AN ENDLESS JOURNEY

We live in a society where silence is a rarity. From the moment of getting up in the morning, radios and televisions are switched on; in every pub, café and shop there is constant muzak, while so many people are locked into their phones. Silence, therefore, has become a rare experience.

But there are two kinds of silence: dead silence and a living silence. Quaker meetings are centred on silence. People sit for an hour in silence unless someone is moved to stand up to say a few words and then sit down again. The most powerful meetings I have attended, however, have been those that were an hour of a silence so vibrant that one is energised in the way that the disciples must have been at Pentecost when tongues of fire descended on everyone's head and all spoke a common language.

The words of secret silence are those that well up from the depths of one's being. As Sean Dunne wrote in *An Irish Spiritual Odyssey*, "monastic silence is closer to the silence of lovers. To live without such inner silence seems like an amputation of some part of myself." In St Mark's Gospel we read how Jesus got up long before dawn, left the house and went off to a lonely place to pray. It was his way of escaping the pressure of people when "the whole town came crowding round the door" and his disciples saying, "Everybody is looking for you." Dame Meinrad Craighead at Stanbrook Abbey once said to me, "The human spirit needs to go off alone – whether you call it praying or not doesn't matter. You find in the quietness there is a harmony, a return to the centre of one's being."

I
HEAR·THESE
WORDS·OF
SECRET
SILENCE:

There was a time when I used to celebrate the Eucharist every Sunday at a tiny church outside Presteigne, in the diocese of Hereford. In the small congregation there was always Becky. Becky was aged about seven, she was the granddaughter of a local farmer and she always came with her old nanny. Becky had difficulty in speaking but had learned to say, "Amen". On one occasion as I was saying the Prayer of Consecration she began to call out, "Amen! Amen! Amen!" I looked up and saw people frowning and I knew I must act swiftly, so I stopped the prayer and joined in, saying, "Amen, Becky! Amen, Amen, Amen!" Immediately everyone's faces lit up with delight rather than disapproval. Becky was included rather than excluded.

:AMEN
AMEN
AMEN
BECKY:

This is a line from a poem by Emily Dickinson and it emphasises the importance of learning to be on one's own. Just as we have to clean our houses at regular intervals and throw out things we no longer need, every now and then we need to take "time out for re-assembly", as Robert Frost once described it.

In my thirties on several occasions I would go to a part of the country I did not know, book a room in a small country pub, and go walking by day. Then at night I would find myself having crucial dreams and, like Theseus, having to face my own shadow side. Each of us has to enter our own labyrinth from time to time to deal with our dark side, just as Jesus did in those forty days in the desert. And we observe also how often he withdrew to a lonely place to pray. However deep the love of friends and lovers, ultimately we are alone, as in that sentence I quote in my foreword, which was painted on an arch inside the Carmelite Monastery at Golders Green: "At Carmel and at the Judgement I am alone". This is why it is important for each of us, from time to time, to go apart, whether on a formal retreat, or simply on our own.

LONELINESS IS·THE MAKER OF SOULS:

pritchard 2020

This is Emily Dickinson again. There are times in our lives — whether it be due to bereavement, some other loss, or deep failure — when the night seems endless. But instead of despairing, we must look at all possible ways of solving our dilemma.

Only in this way, by exploring every possibility, will we find the way through the darkness. Knock and it will open! It is a matter of finding the right door.

———————

NOTKNOWING
WHEN·THE
DAWN
WILL·COME·I
OPEN·EVERY
DOOR ·.

These are the words that Jesus spoke to a man who had been crippled for thirty-eight years and who lay by the pool at Bethesda, hoping to be cured. What Jesus is saying is, "Do you really want to recover?" That may seem a strange question but Jesus, with his profound insight into people, knew that in spite of the man's sincere longing to be well, there was a deep fear of the consequence of health. This is the human dilemma: we cling to what is familiar, however painful, rather than risk change.

Healing is more than curing physical symptoms. The word "heal" is rooted in an older word, "hale", meaning whole. To be healed in Jesus' understanding is to be made whole, not only on a physical level but mentally, emotionally and spiritually. To be healed, says Jesus, you must become a whole person "with all thy heart, with all thy soul, with all thy mind".

Jesus' response to pain and sickness was always one of spontaneous compassion but, deep down, he knew that the cause of sickness lies all too often within the individual. We create our own diseases. Many diseases today are caused by stress, and when we fall ill our body is signalling that something is wrong with our lifestyle and only if we remove that cause will we be well. If only the physical symptoms are treated then, in due course, the body will manifest new symptoms.

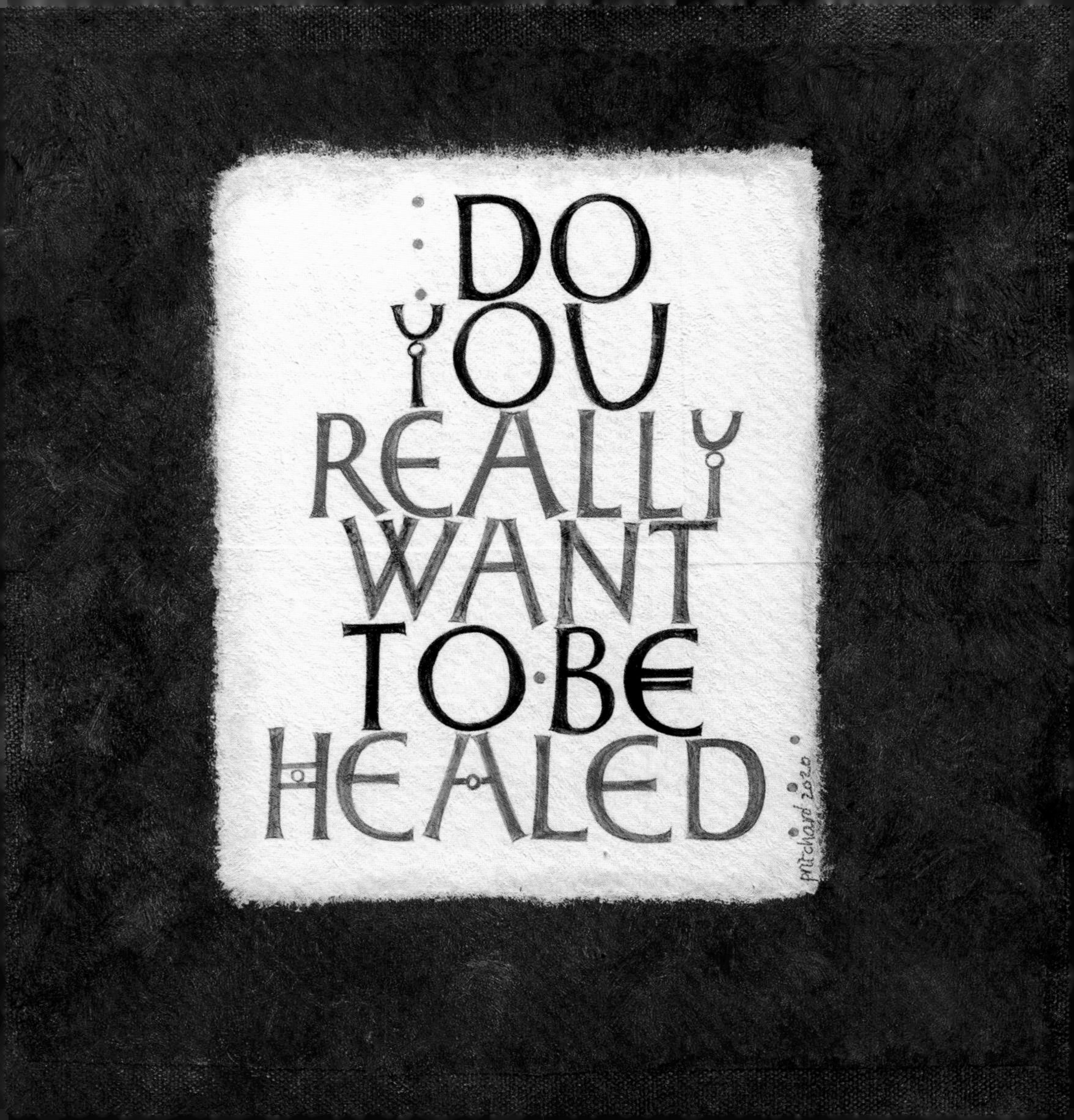
DO
YOU
REALLY
WANT
TO·BE
HEALED
pritchard 2020

These are the words of the mantra that I repeat mentally during meditation, but also at intervals throughout the day, walking to the shops or sitting on a bus. Also in the night, when I wake – which is frequent – I say it, even sometimes whispering it into the dark.

A mantra acts as a lifeline. People may choose just one word for their mantra, or a phrase, but often a mantra will well up from our subconscious and when this happens we must heed it. This is how my mantra came to me. I used to regularly visit my friend Ann Powell who was in her mid-nineties and housebound, and who lived at Great Oak, Eardisley in Herefordshire. One day after leaving her I was standing in the porch when these words came to me unbidden. They are not mine, and because always the gift must move, I know that others have taken these phrases also as their mantra.

There is another aspect to these three sentences. It is as though an important visitor is expected, then the doorbell rings and they have arrived: *God is present*. We open the door and invite them inside: *God is here*. And now comes the interesting part. We can't just stand there; some action is required. And so we lead our guest into the centre room and ask if they would like coffee, tea, wine or just to sit in the garden – for the phrase *God is now* indicates action.

And this is central to the practice of meditation. We do not do it solely for ourselves, which would result in a Cheshire cat-like complacency, but our meditation must flow always into action, what the Buddha called compassion for all sentient beings.

18

GOD·IS
PRESENT

·

GOD·IS
HERE

·

GOD·IS
NOW

Jesus had less than three years in which to do the work he was born to do; the previous thirty years having been a preparation for his mission. Each of us is also born into this world for a purpose, with a blueprint of the life we are meant to live. If at the end of our days we too can say these words, then we can die knowing our work is completed. Sadly all too many never realise their full potential.

I·HAVE·DONE
THE·WORK
YOU·GAVE
ME·TO·DO:

When Mary and Joseph take their child to the Temple to be blessed, Simeon not only foretells the future of the child but says these words to Mary. They apply also to each one of us when our own hearts are broken, our hopes dashed to the ground, sudden disaster strikes, perhaps loss of employment, or of a relationship. If we accept such setbacks in a positive way – what have I to learn from this? – we shall grow deeper in compassion towards others. Those who have been bereaved, for example, are better able to support others during the months of their bereavement. It is those who have been wounded who make the best healers.

A·SWORD·SHALL
PIERCE·YOUR
SOUL·THAT·THE
SECRETS·OF
MANY·HEARTS
SHALL·BE
REVEALED:

We know very little about Mary. It is her silence that is so compelling. Only once, when Jesus has begun his mission, does she seek to intervene and he rebukes her, saying, "Woman, what have I to do with thee?" Thereafter, nothing. And at the end, when his male followers desert him, we know that his mother and the other Mary keep watch at the foot of the cross, hearing the cries of other Jews hanging from crosses. The silence of Mary, the mother of Jesus, is so powerful that it is not surprising that in due course she became the archetypal mother of mankind, recalling the mysterious figure of Sophia, who we read was with God at the beginning of the world. And so we say: Hail Mary, full of grace, the Lord is with thee. Blessed art thou among women and blessed is the fruit of thy womb, Jesus. Holy Mary, Mother of God, pray for us sinners now and at the hour of our death.

MARY
HELD·ALL·THESE
THINGS·IN·HER
HEART:

It is with these words that many prayers end, but they carry an unexpected meaning. Jesus' great mission was to reveal God, not as the angry, jealous Father of the Old Testament, demanding sacrifices, but as a loving parent, both Mother and Father. His abiding image is that of a God of love. And so when we say the words "through Jesus Christ our Lord" it is as though Jesus is a window through which we most clearly see the true nature of God. In this sense Jesus is like a window cleaner!

THROUGH
JESUS·CHRIST
OUR·LORD:

A tree is a rich subject for meditation. Its roots go deep into the ground while the trunk soars up to the sky and its branches spread outwards to provide shelter. We need to learn how to sink our roots deep, while reaching up towards the light, our arms reaching out to embrace our neighbour. Just as the sturdiness of a tree provides a base for birds to build their nests, we too, if our roots are truly deep, can provide a centre to which others may come and share their problems. We can't always be expected to solve those problems, but it is often simple to listen attentively.

I recall when I was preparing for the priesthood at Glasshampton Monastery, Brother Gregory, one of the Franciscan friars, told me how he had been asked by the headmaster of a top public school if he would see a boy of sixteen, from a very good family, who was heavily into drugs. Brother Gregory saw the boy for an hour. Three weeks later he received a letter from the headmaster, thanking him and saying, "I don't know what you said, but the boy is totally changed." Brother Gregory smiled as he told me this. "The thing is," he said, "I didn't say anything. I just listened!" Clearly it was the quality of his listening, his total concentration on what the boy was telling him, which acted as a mirror in which the boy could see himself for the first time.

.

A
TREE
BEING
MOTIONLESS
BIRDS
COME
TO
IT
.
.
.

Jesus said, "Wherever two or three of you are gathered together in my name, there I am in the midst of you." Sadly this is not something that can always be felt in church when we gather for the Eucharist. It is easier to feel this presence in a contemplative setting such as the celebration of Mass at Taizé which involves a lot of silence than in a noisier parish Mass. It is no wonder that Taizé still attracts thousands of young people. Ultimately, however, God is within each one of us. If we kneel before the Blessed Sacrament, although our eyes are focused on the tabernacle, we become aware of the presence of Christ within us. Each of us is a tabernacle for the living God.

I·AM
IN·THE
MIDST
OF·YOU:

We live in a society that is saturated with words and I am reminded of those words of T.S. Eliot: "Where is the wisdom lost in knowledge? Where is the knowledge lost in information?" But some words can also leap off the page, setting us on fire, as in all great poetry such as the Psalms. It is these kind of words that John Rowlands-Pritchard brings to life in the shape and colour of his depiction of them.

Words are even more powerful when chanted, as in many religious houses and monasteries, but also when spoken by someone who has a deep feeling for words, knowing where to pause, or when to inflect a particular word. The choir mistress of Stanbrook Abbey once said to me: "Most clergy read the scriptures like a laundry list!" All clergy need to work on their voices, to strengthen and broaden their vocal range, not to mention the importance of projecting the voice. Today it is assumed that the microphone will do all that for one. This is a total fallacy. What a world away from the days of John Donne preaching in St Paul's Cathedral to a vast congregation who stood, or when John Wesley would preach to hundreds in the open air.

One has only to think of the speeches of Martin Luther King which set his listeners on fire, and how Churchill by his superb oratory brought hope to our country at its lowest ebb. As Jesus said, "I am come to send fire on the earth; and what will I, if it be already kindled?" *Luke 12:49*

Strangely, though we see many statues of the Buddha laughing, we rarely see a painting of Jesus laughing. It was the actor Alec McCowen who, in his brilliant one-man performance of the *Gospel of St Mark*, brought out the humour of Jesus, as well as his exasperation with the obtuseness of his disciples. In many of his stories we can see something of Jesus' humour, while the fact that he was able to mix with such a variety of people must have meant a lively sense of fun. It is all too easy to take oneself too seriously! This is why, especially as one gets older, it is good to be teased. It stops one from becoming pompous! Furthermore, it enables us to see ourselves more objectively.

BLESSED ARE THOSE WHO CAN LAUGH AT THEMSELVES FOR THEY WILL HAVE ENDLESS AMUSEMENT

BLESSED·ARE·THOSE
WHO·CAN·LAUGH·AT
THEMSELVES·FOR·
THEY·WILL·HAVE·END-
-LESS·AMUSEMENT:

This is by Virginia Woolf and it is a haunting passage in its evocation of our journey in life. However deeply loved we are, there are times when we have to travel alone. This, of course, is what so many fear – simply being alone. As Emily Dickinson wrote,

> I fear me this – is Loneliness –
> The Maker of the soul
> Its Caverns and its Corridors
> Illuminate – or seal –

If, however, we are prepared to spend time alone, we will experience returning to our roots. In this silence many problems quietly resolve themselves. We experience a deep movement of inner peace welling up in us so that we are less swept away by emotions of despair or over-excitement. We learn to surf the crests and the hollows.

WE DO NOT KNOW OUR OWN SOULS, LET ALONE THE SOULS OF OTHERS. HUMAN BEINGS DO NOT GO HAND IN HAND THE WHOLE WAY. THERE IS A VIRGIN FOREST IN EACH, A SNOWFIELD WHERE EVEN THE PRINT OF BIRDS' FEET IS UNKNOWN. HERE WE GO ALONE

WE·DO·NOT·KNOW·OUR·OWN
SOULS·LET·ALONE·THE·SOULS
OF·OTHERS·HUMAN·BEINGS
DO·NOT·GO·HAND·IN·HAND
THE·WHOLE·WAY·THERE·IS·A
VIRGIN·FOREST·IN·EACH·A
SNOWFIELD·WHERE·EVEN
THE·PRINT·OF·BIRDS·FEET·IS
UNKNOWN·HERE·WE·GO
ALONE

Once, in Colorado Springs, I was teaching a course at Colorado College on the creation of new rituals. At one point I invited the students to write a prayer to a known or unknown God. This is what one of them wrote:

> With the unsecuring sea stretching
> Before me,
> To mystery
> I make my pledge.
> To searching
> To swim
> To dive as deep as I can.
>
> With the unsecuring sea stretching
> Before me,
> To mystery
> I give my thanks
> For you I am thankful
> With you I am
> Without you I am not.

For those who have the courage to make such a commitment, who are prepared to search, to dive as deep as they can, they will always find the sunken treasure hidden deep within themselves and, like Walt Whitman, be enabled to say, "Now in a moment I know what I am for and a thousand songs spring to life within my breast!"

PUT·OUT·INTO
THE·DEEP·AND
LET·DOWN
YOUR·NETS
FOR·A·CATCH:

An old nursery rhyme reads:

> A wise old owl lived in an oak;
> The more he saw, the less he spoke;
> The less he spoke, the more he heard.
> Why can't we all be like that wise old bird?

When people spill out their problems to us it's often tempting to rush in with solutions whereas, as every wise analyst knows, the individual has to find his or her own answers. Always the less said the better! But we can, by gentle questioning, sometimes help the individual to find a solution. "Why do you think this is? Why do you think so-and-so acted in this way?" But no more than that.

THE MORE HE
SAW·THE·LESS
HE·SPOKE·THE
LESS·HE·SPOKE
THE·MORE·HE
HEARD·

These are the words of Thomas Merton on the last day of his life, as he joined hands in a circle of prayer with Christian and Buddhist monks. He said:

> We are going to have to create a new language of prayer and this new language has to come out of something which transcends all our traditions and comes out of the immediacy of Love. That love can only be found in prayer. It is a matter of growth, deepening, and of an ever greater love and grace in our hearts. Never was it more necessary for us to respond to that action. I pray that we may all do so.

It means also facing much in ourselves that is ugly or discordant – jealousies, resentments, lusts, angers – and, by acknowledging them, tame them. Dag Hammarskjöld, former Secretary-General of the United Nations, wrote in his journal: "Now, when I have overcome my fears of others, of myself, at the frontier of the unheard-of. Here ends the known. But from a source beyond it, something fills my being with its possibilities – at the frontier."

THE·REAL·JOURNEY·IN·LIFE·IS·INTERIOR:

This line from Samuel Beckett reminds one of Jesus' remark that no man, having put his hand to the plough and turned back, is worthy of the kingdom of God. Once we commit ourselves to the inner spiritual journey in whatever form, we continue day in, day out; in fair weather, storms, hail or frost. If we meditate there will be times when we suffer from many distractions and idle thoughts, buzzing like bluebottle flies, so that we will often be tempted to give up. But no, we persevere in season and out of season. It is as a Desert Father observed: "I rise up and I fall down. I rise up and I fall down. I rise up and I fall down."

I·CAN'T
GO·ON·I
MUST·GO
ON·I·WILL
GO·ON

Herman Hesse, in his novel *Journey to the East*, describes the many pilgrimages made over the centuries and realises that each and every one is travelling home. We come from God and we go to God. However different, each route leads to the same destination.

It was this image that inspired Pope John Paul II to invite the leaders of all the world religions to join him in Assisi in 1986 to pray for world peace. Among those attending were the Dalai Lama, the Archbishop of Canterbury, Metropolitan Filaret of the Russian Orthodox Church, the President of the Shinto Shrine Association of Tokyo, plus Buddhists, Jains, Jews, Hindus, Muslims, Sikhs and Zoroastrians – some 150 religious leaders in all. Senior Vatican officials said that never before had such an array of religious figures participated in a single event.

Interestingly, that most aristocratic of popes, Pope Pius XII, said at a gathering of cardinals, "The Roman Church must not seek to embrace the entire world. It must learn to accept that there are other faiths, other creeds, other temperaments." And in 1998 Pope John Paul II observed in a general audience, "The Second Vatican Council teaches that 'the Catholic Church rejects nothing of what is true and holy in non-Christian religions. Although the routes may be different, there is but a single goal to which is directed the deepest aspiration of the human spirit as expressed in its quest for God... for the full meaning of life.'"

ALWAYS GOING HOME :: WHERE ARE WE REALLY

There are various ways of meditating. The Buddhist practice of mindfulness consists of counting one's ingoing and outgoing breath through the nostrils eight times. On the first breath we mentally count "one", pause, and then "one" again on exhaling. On the next breath we count "two" and so on. If we lose count then we have to go back to the beginning and start all over again!

The other main form of meditation is the use of a mantra, which is a word or phrase that is meaningful to the individual. One of our meditation group, on learning that her husband had Parkinson's and realising she would be sorely tried, took the words "That I may be filled with loving kindness" as her mantra over the next twelve years of his life. Whatever the word or phrase, the regular repetition of it sinks deep into the unconscious, becoming embedded in our psyches. We become filled with loving kindness.

THAT I MAY
BE FILLED
WITH LOVING
KINDNESS:

We are besieged by a swarm of distracting thoughts like a plague of mosquitoes but, even more, by what Eckhart Tolle in *The Power of Now* calls "the pain body". Our body develops aches, twinges, itches, anything to distract us from sitting still and allowing our minds to calm down! Even practised meditators experience this and the strong temptation is to give up, either for that day or for good.

Here the story of Ulysses is very relevant. Ulysses, returning to Ithaca after the Trojan war, is warned by Circe that when his ship passes the island of the Sirens, his crew must block their ears with wax and fasten Ulysses to the mast with ropes. The Sirens are beautiful women with amazing voices who promise all delights, but any who succumb are killed. Ulysses, strongly tempted, strains at his bonds, but is enabled to sail on. So we, seated alone in the silence, must acknowledge the many distractions but let them go. If we persevere we will reach a still centre which is where the Divine is to be found. Seek and ye shall find!

34

ALL·OF
HUMANITYS
PROBLEMS
STEM·FROM
MANS
INABILITY·TO
SIT·QUIETLY
IN·A·ROOM
ALONE:

pritchard 2020

When people buy one of my books on meditation and ask me to write something in it, I always add these words, for it is when we walk the same route day after day that we create a path. And so it is with the practice of meditation. We simply have to make a start and then persevere, day in and day out, season after season. I have been meditating for over fifty years and still there are days when distractions buzz like bees from a swarm, but I persevere. It is by persevering that, over time, an inner citadel of peace is created.

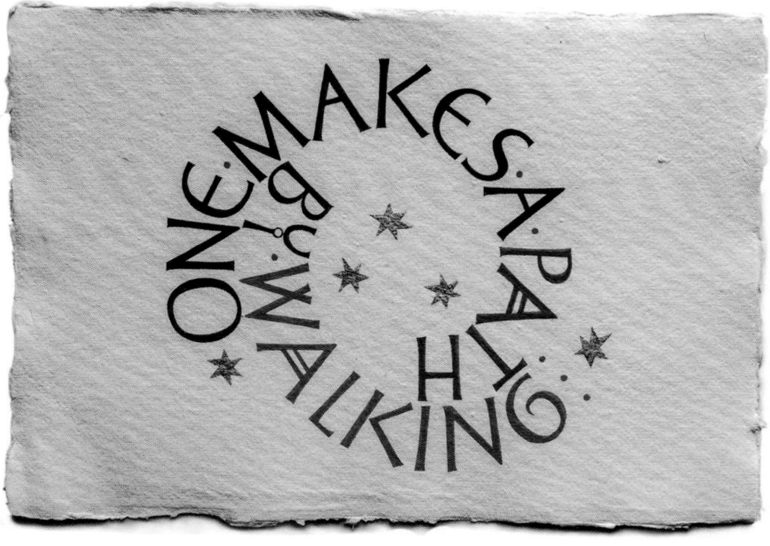
ONE·MAKES·A·PATH·BY·WALKING

This is one of the Desert Fathers speaking to a young monk. Similarly Jesus counsels that we go into a room, shut the door, and be alone. In a world of endless distractions and noise we will never find an inner peace unless we go apart into a lonely place. It is as simple as that! In India, where often whole families live in one room, there will be a corner curtained off, and when any member of the family goes into that corner they all know that she or he has gone to meditate.

GO·TO·YOUR
CELL·YOUR
CELL·WILL
TEACH·YOU
EVERYTHING·

I don't know the origin of this phrase but it has acted as a lodestar throughout my life. Recently, now in my ninety-third year, I remarked on this to a friend who replied, "but surely innocence means naivety?" It can, of course, but for me it means being open to experience.

In Joyce Carey's book *Art and Reality*, he has a description of a small child of seven who once asked him if he would like a drawing of a swan. For half an hour she sat drawing the most original swan he had ever seen. It was a swimming swan. Its feet were enormous and very carefully finished, obviously from life. The whole structure of the feet was shown in heavy black lines. The child was used to watching swans on a canal at the bottom of her garden and had taken particular notice of the feet. Below the water the swan was all power. But for the body she gave it the faintest, lightest outline, neck and wings included in one round line shaped rather like a cloud. He was admiring this swan when her older sister observed, "That's not a swan! I'll draw you a swan," and then produced a Christmas card type of swan. Yet, as Carey observed, the second child had all the qualities of the first but had lost it by the education which emphasises facts, measurements, the concept. And the concept is always the enemy of intuition. It is said that when you give a child the name of a bird, it loses the bird. It never sees the bird again, but only a sparrow, a thrush, a swan. We fix the label and then cease looking.

37

:KEEP
INNOCENCY:

These words are by an eighth-century Buddhist scholar and they remind us of the Dalai Lama's observation that the practice of meditation should result in a greater awareness of others and their needs. As Jesus said to his friends in his hour of greatest need, "Could you not watch with me one hour?" How many of us actually pause at intervals throughout the day in order to rest, if only for a moment, in the eternal silence? Do we take time to reflect on the day's events and encounters? Do we listen for the subtext of what people are trying to say to us? The more we listen to the silence within, the more we shall begin to hear the silence in other people. The inner life of prayer and meditation is not a self-enclosed garden only for our own delight. Once we have found the way to the centre, our lives will become like an open garden.

MAY·I·BE
A·BOAT·A
BRIDGE·A
PASSAGE
FOR·THOSE
DESIRING
THE·OTHER
SHORE·

This is a line from Shakespeare's *Hamlet* in which Hamlet uses not the word God but "Divinity", meaning a God-like energy which, however much we muck things up, shapes our individual lives. In other words, there is to each life a definite pattern and purpose. The way this unfolds is called "synchronicity". We have only to reflect on those occasions when we have taken down a book at random and it falls open at a passage that relates directly to whatever is our current dilemma. Similarly at key moments in our lives certain individuals appear to point us in the way we should go, or draw us back from taking a wrong path.

Synchronistic events impart a sense of being part of a greater whole; we discern an underlying pattern. But to be aware of this pattern we need to practise silence. It is revealing how in his hugely demanding role as only the second Secretary-General of the United Nations, Dag Hammarskjöld regularly meditated each day.

39

THERE·IS·A
DIVINITY
WHICH·SHAPES
OUR·ENDS
ROUGH·HEW
THEM·HOW
WE·WILL·

WHEN TRUE SIMPLICITY IS GAINED,
TO BOW AND TO BEND
WE SHAN'T BE ASHAMED.
TO TURN, TURN, WILL BE OUR DELIGHT
TILL BY TURNING, TURNING, WE COME ROUND RIGHT

These words are from the Shaker hymn *Simple Gifts*, the melody of which was used by Sydney Carter for his famous hymn *Lord of the Dance*. The Shakers in their worship used to spin and turn, emphasising the need always to be open to change, to yield, to grow. The words of the hymn end "Till by turning, turning, we come round right". I recall leading a day workshop on the Shakers and recreating their form of worship. One of those present, a physiotherapist who worked at a hospice in Hereford, commented how those individuals who had learned to yield to many smaller deaths in their lives – the death of a child or loved one, the death of an ambition, and so on – had the easiest deaths, whereas those who had fought against every change had the hardest deaths, unable to let go. We have to learn how to be flexible and grow through change.

This is from the fifth-century martyr Boethius:

> Thou art the journey and the journey's end.
> To see Thee is the end and the beginning.
> Thou carriest us and Thou dost go before.
> Thou art the journey and the journey's end.

As the Sufi mystic Rumi wrote, "We come from God and we go to God." Those who know this deep within themselves have therefore no fear of dying. We are never alone but surrounded by an eternal love. But this is not a knowledge that can be acquired by studying texts; it has to be experienced in the deep silence of prayer. What is not always understood is that there are three forms of knowledge. There is scientific knowledge, which is the weighing of one fact against another; there is philosophic knowledge, which is the weighing of one argument against another; and finally, there is intuitive knowledge, which comes from an unknown source and is the inspiration of all great artists from Shakespeare to Bach. It is, as Thomas Aquinas learned in his final vision, a knowledge that is beyond words. No wonder that Hamlet's last words are "The rest is silence."

This is a Celtic prayer which carries one safely into the night. Lying in the darkness we murmur these words and commend ourselves to that eternal love which ever surrounds and upholds us. One has only to murmur these words and then sink into the deep waters of sleep.

42

:THOU·BEING·OF
MARVELS:
ENCOMPASS
ME·THIS·NIGHT
BOTH·SOUL·AND
BODY:COMPASS
ME·THIS·NIGHT
AND·ON·EVERY
NIGHT:

Always when staying in a monastery my favourite moment is when, after Compline, the community sing the *Salve Regina*:

> Hail, Holy Queen, Mother of Mercy. Hail our life, our sweetness and our hope. To thee do we cry, poor banished children of Eve. To thee do we send up our sighs, mourning and weeping in this vale of tears. Turn then, most gracious advocate, thine eyes of mercy towards us, and after this our exile show unto us the blessed fruit of thy womb, Jesus. O clement, O loving, O sweet Virgin Mary.

The monks then blow out their candles, raise their hoods over their heads and quietly leave the abbey church for the Great Silence. It is indeed fitting that, as night falls, we commend ourselves into the keeping of the Eternal Mother who watches over us all. She is not only Mary, the mother of Jesus, but Sophia, the figure of Wisdom, of whom we read that she was with God at the creation of the world.

THEN IN THE SECRET PLACE OF MY HEART TEACH ME WISDOM

This verse from the Psalms emphasises the importance of the heart rather than the head or brain. In India it is taught that in the heart a small flame burns and the task of spiritual practice and meditation is to keep that flame alight. As the Bhagavad Gita teaches, "the soul is like a lamp whose light is steady, for it burns in a shelter where no winds come". It is in this deep silence that we begin to find the answers to the three most important questions: who am I; where have I come from; where am I going?

44

THEN·IN·THE
SECRET·PLACE
OF·MY·HEART
TEACH·ME
WISDOM

It was once a custom to light a candle in the window on Christmas Eve, as in this verse:

Open the door tonight
within your heart and light
the lantern of love there to shine afar.
On a tumultuous sea
some straining craft maybe,
with bearings lost, shall sight love's silver star.

YOU SHALL LIGHT MY CANDLE, YOU MAKE MY
DARKNESS TO BE LIGHT

YOU·SHALL
LIGHT·MY
CANDLE·
YOU·MAKE·MY
DARKNESS
TO·BE·LIGHT

PSALM·VERSE

PRICHARD·2012

These words remind us that the cracks which so often disfigure our lives – whether cracks of betrayal, disillusion, failure, or pain – are often the means by which the light of eternity breaks through, so that we begin to see things from a different perspective. As George Herbert wrote,

> Who would have thought my shriveled heart
> Could have recovered greenness? It was gone
> Quite underground; as flowers depart
> To feed their mother root when they have blown;
> Where they together
> All the hard weather,
> Dead to the world, keep house unknown.

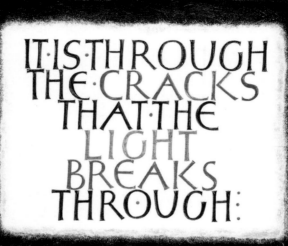

IT IS THROUGH
THE CRACKS
THAT THE
LIGHT
BREAKS
THROUGH:

During the years of my Jungian analysis I was encouraged to draw or paint my dreams or feelings, and this has stood me in good stead. I recall one period in my life when I did not know which way I was meant to go. I began to draw a deep well, which was totally dried up, with myself trapped at the bottom with no way out; an image perfectly revealing of the state I was in. My pencil hovered and then began to draw a small opening at the bottom of the well, which I realised I was meant to crawl through. My pencil then drew a cave and small stone altar on which was a single seed. It was then that I understood this was the seed of meditation, which I had been neglecting, and that my task was to water it daily. And so I returned to the daily practice of silent meditation. This line from the Psalms reminds us also that God is a well that never runs dry. We have but to lower a bucket and draw up grace and strength from below.

WITH·YOU
IS·THE
WELL
OF·LIFE :

Cardinal Basil Hume used to say to his people who were dying: "Soon after you are dead – we're not sure how long – you will be united with the most ecstatic love you've ever known. As one of the best things in your life was human love, this will be love, but much more satisfying, and it will last forever."

THE GATEWAY TO·PERFECT LOVE:

pritchard 2020

Loneliness is increasingly a symptom of the times we live in. In the UK some 7.7 million people live alone, while 5 million people over seventy-five say their only company is the television. Loneliness has also been found to be endemic among those between the ages of twenty-four and thirty-four. In addition to this, we know that children, while more digitally connected than any previous generation, are increasingly feeling alone and isolated. They can have a thousand Facebook friends but not one with a flesh-and-blood face.

As St Teresa of Calcutta said, "I know the greatest suffering in the world is being lonely, feeling unloved, just having no one. I have come more and more to realise that it is being unwanted that is the worst disease today that any human being can experience, being unwanted." It is because, as a society, we have lost the sense of being part of a community.

It is, however, when a group of people are gathered together to meditate or pray that the silence can become so vibrant that we know God is in our midst. This is why, for many Christians, gathering in small house groups, even once a month, can be a rich experience. God is present. God is here. God is now.

WHERE TWO OR THREE ARE GATHERED TOGETHER IN MY NAME THERE I AM IN THE MIDST OF THEM:

pritchard 2020

To love is to be vulnerable, to be open to one another. The tabernacle of God is within but God is also made manifest in each one of us. Each one of us is the Church but, even more, each one of us is our own church. In any congregation how many truly relate to one another as well as to those outside? We live in a society which has lost the sense of neighbourliness, of reaching out to help one another. We need to be reminded that one of the two commands that Jesus left us is "Love thy neighbour as thyself!"

IF·YOU·HAVE
LOVE
FOR·ONE
ANOTHER
THEN·ALL
WILLKNOW
YOU·ARE·MY
DISCIPLES ::

A man was knocked down in an car accident in New York. While waiting for an ambulance, one of the bystanders took off her coat, rolled it up and placed it under his head. "Are you comfortable?" she asked. He replied, "I make a good living." Many make a good living, but whether they have really lived is another matter. A mother may say to her son, "I'd be so proud if you were a lawyer", when perhaps the son wants to be a carpenter. So he goes off and becomes a lawyer but, at the end of his life, he may say, "I made a good living, but I have never lived. I could have been such a good carpenter but my family didn't want that."

Each one of us has our own story to tell, one life to live, one song to sing. The deep fear of many is less that of physical death than that of dying with their song unsung. Each one of us has a unique story and we cannot discover our deepest meaning unless we learn how to live it, so that at the end of our days we can, like Jesus, say, "I have done the work which Thou gavest me to do." It is often in the silence of meditation that we hear the first notes of our own song. Having heard it, it is up to us, in the famous words of Joseph Campbell, "to follow our bliss".

These are words by the Sufi master Llewellyn Vaughan-Lee from his book *Catching the Thread*. "For every seeker," he writes, "the spiritual path will be different. Every lover makes their own unique pilgrimage within the heart. And He loves us for our own individual self. He loves the fact that we are different because He made us different. In this love affair there can be neither comparison nor competition. We each must find our own way of loving Him, of being with Him." We have only to look at the lives of the saints, from St Teresa of Calcutta to St Francis of Assisi, to individuals such as Elizabeth Fry or Abbé Pierre to realise the truth of this.

HEART: LOVE & WITHIN MAKES THEIR OWN PILGRIM UNIQUE EVERY THE A

prtulleul 2020

James Roose-Evans is one of Britian's most experienced and innovative theatre directors, and has directed in the West End, on Broadway, in Paris and in Athens. His dramatisation and production of Helene Hanff's *84 Charing Cross Road* won him awards on both sides of the Atlantic for Best Play and Best Director. He founded the Hampstead Theatre in London, and also, on the Welsh Borders, The Bleddfa Centre for the Creative Spirit.

Beyond the stage, James is a non-stipendiary priest of the Anglican Church, the author of twenty-one books and a blog of thoughts and inspirations **www.jamesrooseevans.co.uk**.

In 2020 at Lambeth Palace he was presented by the Archbishop of Canterbury with the Dunstan Award for Prayer and the Religious Life, for his contribution to exploring over sixty-five years the relationship between art and life, the creative and the spiritual.